R H O D A   B A

# MOMENTS

*An Inspirational Devotional Journal:*
Stories and Words to Inspire, Confront, and Conquer Everyday Life Situation

*AuthorHouse™*
*1663 Liberty Drive*
*Bloomington, IN 47403*
*www.authorhouse.com*
*Phone: 1 (800) 839-8640*

*Published by AuthorHouse 02/16/2018*

*ISBN: 978-1-5462-2956-8 (sc)*
*ISBN: 978-1-5462-2958-2 (hc)*
*ISBN: 978-1-5462-2957-5 (e)*

*Print information available on the last page.*

authorHOUSE®

This inspirational journal and devotional is dedicated to my mother, affectionately known as Dorothy, who departed this life way before those who loved her were ready to see her go. And to my three sisters, Rhoshay, Rayneika, and Rayshaun, who Dorothy raised to be independent, resilient, and full of faith, just like her.

# Contents

# Foreword

Moments. They range from the routine and mundane to the extraordinary and transformational. Moments. We experience moments every day, at various times during the day, yet how often do we intentionally pause to fully absorb and take note of these moments?

I'd like to share such a moment with you.

As I sat there in the lobby, anticipating, waiting, I had a notion I was about to experience a transformational moment. And I was right. As I sat there facing forward, looking outside toward the parking lot, trying to enjoy the moment—which can be a challenge for me—I decided to enjoy this moment. I forced myself to find something to enjoy in the moment even when I knew I was about to enter what I knew would undoubtedly be a string of stressful moments. Question after question after question. It was about to happen. I focused on the sun, although I could not see the sun itself, I focused on its rays streaming down through moving openings in the tree canopy.

Then I heard it: the click of the lobby door being unlocked, followed by an energetic push of the big, glass door swinging toward me, and then a delightful, joy-filled voice as I looked up and to my right. "You must be Bridget … I'm Rhoda!" This first moment happened in August of 2014. This first moment was, without a doubt, a God-ordained moment that has led to many other profoundly impactful and blessed moments.

I was there for a job interview. Subsequently, Rhoda hired me into a newly created position on her staff. Shortly after I began working for Rhoda, she let me know she likely would not be my leader for much longer, and she was right. A few months after I started, Rhoda accepted a new role and moved on to her new opportunity. In the short time we worked together, we developed a deep, authentic friendship, which is often very rare at this stage of life—another confirmation that God designed our paths to cross at a very specific time.

I have shared a great deal of my life story with Rhoda, and likewise, she has shared a great deal with me. Because Rhoda has beckoned and drawn me into her life, I have had the sacred opportunity to witness firsthand, up close and personal, Rhoda live through some of the moments you will read about in the following pages.

When I say Rhoda has beckoned and drawn me into her life, it has been more like a pursuing embrace, almost as if she has been put on assignment. I am one who is not easy to get to know. I'm a proud, unapologetic introvert, which means I go for depth and meaningful connection with a select few rather than lots of social activity with many.

What Rhoda has done for me—outside of mentoring and encouraging me, listening to me and challenging me, celebrating and pushing me—is she has reminded me in a very tangible way of how Christ pursues us. She has demonstrated to me God's love during a time when I felt forgotten, overlooked, and as if I were blending in with the scenery of life. She has called out the gifts that she sees in me and often put me front and center when everything within me was screaming, "I'm not ready yet!"

This book is not about me, yet I would not feel right if I did not take the time to acknowledge the exponential growth I have experienced personally, professionally, and spiritually since Rhoda has come into my life. To say my life has been richly blessed does not do it justice.

One thing that Rhoda and I have in common is that we have both been closet, unpublished writers for many years. Our public writings have mostly gone unnoticed or noted as par for the course. I've written curriculum for professional development and graduate course work. I've written speeches and talking points for executives—presidents, vice presidents, directors. I've sat as a silent witness in the audience while they mixed the words I have written with their own personalities. There is a certain feeling I get when I sit and hear the words I've written being spoken by someone else. I've helped, and that is where I get fulfillment. It gives me great joy to help people craft, develop, and fine-tune a message they want to get across to their audience—whether that message is to thank employees for their dedication, their service, their loyalty to the mission, or whether that message is about why the organization needs to make reductions and cut backs. I am often invited to the table to help fine-tune or write the message from scratch. I'm anonymous. Author's name? Not important. It's the message and, more important, the people who are affected by the message who are most important.

I have private, personal, unpublished writings as well. Writings that have only been shared with two people, one of whom is Rhoda. Rhoda knows my desire to one day share my writings, my stories, in a transparent, public way, in the hopes my story will encourage someone. And this—what I've written here—is an example of me getting Rhoda-ed! In one moment, I'm celebrating and cheering her on with every update she shares about the journey to publishing her first book. Then she one day sends me an e-mail asking, "Will you write the foreword for my book?"

My logical, internal response was, "No! You should get somebody else. Somebody who at least ten people know. No one knows me. Writing someone's foreword is a huge responsibility. People will skip past the foreword." But just as fast as that negative loop started to play, I heard Rhoda's voice, "When you have an opportunity before you, no matter how ill-equipped and unprepared you feel, say yes." So, I replied and made my fingers type, "I would be honored." Because this is an honor. I have the honor, especially if you do not know Rhoda, of introducing you to her, her message, and her gift.

You will see in the following pages, Rhoda writes from a place of vulnerability and experienced joy and pain. We all experience these moments, but how many of us take the time to capture them, write them down, and then take it one step further and share those moments? Open. Vulnerable. Not too many of us do this or else there'd be many more published writers in the world.

Most of us tend to share our lives in a very choosy fashion—carefully cultivated and sculptured. On social media, we share the perfected, filtered selfie: the happy, clean, and compartmentalized parts of our lives. Or, we do the opposite. We overshare, sharing everything, from the emotion we're feeling at this exact moment to our lunch plates, how our neighbor took up two parking spots again, in rapid succession. It's an overabundance and overwhelming amount of moments.

Here, Rhoda shares a few select moments. However, make no mistake: while they are selected moments, they are the full spectrum. They are open and unfiltered in the hopes they will "bless and encourage at least one person," as she says.

Whether you read the devotional in order, cover to cover, or whether you pick up this book and search by topic for whatever it is you are currently experiencing or in need of—hope, despair, inspiration—Rhoda has a word for you.

Now that I've shared how Rhoda has impacted my life, allow me to usher you into Rhoda's sitting room. Rhoda's sitting room is wherever you are—your kitchen table, your office, sitting in your car waiting for your child's football practice to be over, or on a plane in midflight.

Come on in, grab your favorite beverage, have a seat, get comfortable, share, and enjoy a moment with Rhoda.

Bridget Mitchell
Rhoda's Friend

Momma,
    Thank you for always being there for me in every moment.
    Love,
    Bridget
Mar. 20, 2018

# Preface

Moments. We all have them. However, it is those faith-defining moments that disclose where we are in our journey and where we are in our spiritual walk. Faith-defining moments are times or points in our natural lives when we experience some emotion or internal feeling of impact, which are often memorable and reflective. Some moments we experience may leave us with a bruise, some may leave us with a smile, but all leave us with a lesson.

Those profound moments that are distinct and life-altering, those moments we remember, they leave a profound impact within the imprints of our being, becoming a part of who we are.

Those moments hold the most meaning to us. They can come in the form of spoken words, an individual's presence, an event, a situation, etc. Those moments not only test our strength but define our point of view in life and serve as building blocks for how we react, respond, and overcome future moments in life.

We have moments of truth, moments of joy, moments of sadness, moments of strength, moments of fulfillment, moments of insecurity, moments of doubt, moments of faith, moments of guilt, and the list could go on. However, God chose us to experience those moments not simply for our own benefit and learning but so that we can gain the necessary experience required to help others going through their faith-defining moments. While doing so these moments transform into packaged opportunities divinely designed for us to connect directly with God himself. Those moments are purposed to generate time well spent, separated from the natural influences of our current circumstances. We are forever spiritually changed and equipped to complete this walk of life, full of God's divine insight and great wisdom.

This book was inspired by the very idea of connecting with God and sharing with others; this book presented me with a unique opportunity to not only reflect upon the various faith-defining moments I have personally experienced in life; it also allowed me the opportunity to spend precious moments attuned to the voice of the Lord.

I am listening to his kind and gentle words, expressing his love for me, prompting me to share my moments with the world. Through taking the time out to experience my shared moments, I am sharing and experiencing moments with God himself.

In advance, I praise God for your profound and faith-defining moments; I know and believe that they will bring you great joy and great peace! For in one moment, Christ died for our sins and freed us from an inevitable future of continuous moments of darkness and torment.

As you read this book, take a moment to thank God for the plan that he has for you. As you read this book, take a moment to thank God for this very moment, for there are many who have passed through life not recognizing, acknowledging, or embracing their moments. Or they have lived their moments recklessly without care, not realizing the impact or opportunity that each moment had. Over time, moments add up, and the sum of those moments and how we respond to them influence where and how we will spend our future moments in eternity.

Your takeaway is to cherish, embrace, and value your faith-defining moments. Live each moment as though it were your final one; make wise decisions in the moment, take time to reflect, and then chose a reaction that you can look back on and be proud of.

Got a moment? Need a moment? Take a moment, and be inspired.

# Introduction

The purpose and goal of this book is to touch as many lives as possible in an impactful and life-altering way. The words on each page were spoken directly from the voice of God; I was simply the instrument that he used to write them. And through obedience, I share them.

This inspirational devotion is meant to serve as a source for reflection on life's faith-defining moments. I provide the reader with a positive perspective, integrating fragments of my very own life experiences, perspectives, and beliefs and how I chose to respond and react to the trials and everyday challenges of life. You too can choose to respond in a way which is both uplifting and emotionally healthy.

While there are countless classifications of faith-defining moments that we all experience in life, some named and some not yet named, this book is meant to focus on those most common faith-defining moments that every human has or will experience at some point. If you are seeking to learn more about a specific faith-defining moment that is not mentioned within this book, do not be discouraged; apply the same principles that are consistently implied throughout this reading, and you will experience great freedom and joy despite the moment, no matter how great or overwhelmingly challenging your faith-defining moment might be. Your outlook, your perspective, your faith, and your relationship with God will determine how you react to and experience your moments.

# MOMENT OF HOPE

At the present time, we are living in an age when racial matters are highly exposed and our political infrastructure is in question. These current moments present those who believe with the opportunity to pray without ceasing. One would think that those civil rights activists who have fought, marched, and sacrificed their entire lives for equality for all would have led to a better day, a better way. However, just like Jesus, who sacrificed his life for the world, that very act has not yet resulted in a sin-free world. The totality of efforts of those heroes of the past, present, and future will one day be realized.

These uncertain times often lead to a variety of emotions, thoughts, and actions that are not always healthy or productive. However, we who believe must not perpetuate the negativity; we must set the example that demonstrates that we are one body in Christ. The ever-popular biblical statement, "A nation divided will stand," is so very true, and the current state of our world is, unfortunately, living out this reality.

Yet there is hope! If we walk by our faith, if we look to the Lord, the author and finisher of our faith, and if we demonstrate love regardless of how we are being treated, we will overcome this great moment of division. Someone once asked me, "What do you think Dr. Martin Luther King Jr. would say if he were still alive?" I gave this some thought and answered with a poem titled "The Journey to Progress."

## A Poem Pause

"The Journey to Progress"

The journey to progress, while painful and blue, people have come together in unity and truth. The sacrifices made were not in vain, although to this present day, we still experience pain.

Our youth, while portrayed in unpleasant light, it is worth noting that the majority are committed to a positive fight.

I once had a dream that all would be one, not judged by outward appearance but by content of character and no longer shunned.

On the journey to progress, while still miles to go, we have come too far to allow hate, pride, and disparity to stunt our growth.

Many have been called to model the truth; many lives will be lost before we are through.

I once said, "Darkness cannot drive out darkness: only light can do that." My perspective is obviously valid, based on more recent facts.

Homicides are up; respect, love, and forgiveness are down. Now is the time for all to sit down. Take a seat at the table of open dialogue with respect; let's all work together to have a profound and positive effect.

I've been to the mountaintop, and what did I see? I saw peace, love, and harmony. All humankind was treated as one. Our government officials were held in high regard. Our youth were leaders, mentors, men of stature, and more. Our police forces and communities were of one accord, all sharing in the mission to serve and protect once more.

My message is the same: I will not fall back. And we must love our enemies and never attack. We must use our intellect to articulate the facts; we must educate ourselves, lead by example, and give back.

The journey to progress, while it is hard to see, I am still very encouraged and full of belief. We will overcome. I still have a dream. I've been to the mountaintop, and, oh my, what a beautiful scene.

There is always hope! If we look to the author and finisher of our faith and emphasize the positive instead of simply focusing on the negative, hope, joy, and peace will excel. We as a human race will leave a legacy that lives on for future generations, providing them with an anchor and foundation of prosperity.

# Hope Memento

Hope is not helpless. It is full of optimistic strength, making the unbelievable achievable.

## Reflection Moment

Take a moment. Sit quietly and still, listen to the voice of the Lord, and take note of what he is saying to you right now regarding hope. Reflect on past moments, including how you responded and what you can do differently going forward.

### *Reflection Starters*

What has happened in my life when I felt hopeless?

Did I focus too much on the situation? Did I make the situation bigger than God, the creator?

_____

_____

_____

_____

_____

_____

_____

_____

_____

_____

## Scripture Moment

"And his name will be the hope of all the world."
(Matthew 12:21)

Rejoice in our confident hope. Be patient in trouble, and keep on praying.
(Romans 12:12)

# MOMENT OF FEAR

You may be wondering, *Why jump right into such a dark moment?* There is validity for this. Fear is the most universal emotion that every living being has experienced in this life. It is an emotion that, if not properly managed, can dictate how we live every moment on earth.

Fear and faith are opposites. Like darkness and light, the two cannot coexist. To fear something or someone is a sign of unbelief. To face fearful situations is a normal part of life; however, unbeknownst to many, we do not have to yield to fear! Why? When you have accepted the great I AM, creator of heaven and earth, when situations present themselves with fear as a companion, you can reject fear and embrace faith. It's a choice.

I have faced fearful situations in the past and present, and I certainly will in the future! I must be honest and fully transparent; I have failed many of the fear tests. Case in point: my mother was diagnosed with stage 3b lung cancer, an inoperable tumor behind her right lung. I initially chose to reject the fear of watching her go through a painful situation with a high propensity to die at the hand of this horrible disease. Therefore, I stood by her side during her very aggressive treatment plan, and I spoke faith. As days went by, she completed the treatment plan and seemed to be on the road to recovery and back to her energetic self. Then another opportunity presented itself to fear. Three months after completing her treatment, she was scheduled for a CAT scan to confirm how the treatment had affected the tumor. I arrived at the doctor's office with her, after speaking *faith talk* along the way, and the doctor spoke these words: "The treatment did accomplish what we had hoped. The tumor has shrunken significantly. However, the CAT scan now shows multiple nodules in both lungs. This is now what we call stage 4 lung cancer."

Silence.

My mother, who was sitting in a chair against the wall, appeared nonchalant, as if he had not spoken a word. She said nothing, and her expression did not change. I, on the other hand, started to cry. She looked at me and said, "I should have left you at home!"

Shortly after Dorothy—my sisters and I affectionately call her by her first name—spoke those words to me, the nurse entered the room to collect information from my mother for a special blood test and looked confused as to which one of us she should be addressing. Finally, the nurse mustered up the courage and asked, "Now which one of you is the patient?" We all burst into laughter. Here I was, sitting healthy, absent of a diagnosis, with my mother who had been terminally diagnosed, and I was not only hugging fear gently but embracing and holding onto fear for dear life! I quickly reminded myself of my faith and said within, *Lord, help me to believe and to not only talk the talk but to walk the walk!*

My mother, a nonbeliever at that point, took this news regarding her health condition like a champ. We had talked earlier about going to breakfast after the doctor's visit. After we heard the news, received orders from the physician, and prepared to leave, I asked my mother if she was still interested in going to eat. She replied, "Heck yes! I am so hungry!" And so we went.

Days passed, and days will come when fear regarding this very situation will present itself again. I, being a believer, need to walk the talk, stand tall in the face of fear, and say to fear, "I believe!" I must stand in faith no matter what. I must believe, even if Dorothy, my mom, passes on due to this illness. I must have faith in God and believe it is her time, it is God's will, and it is for her soul's salvation. When we put things into perspective, there really is no need to fear. While my example may be perceived as extreme in nature, it is a reality for millions.

If in a life-and-death situation, we can believe instead of fear. Then, certainly, everything and anything else that presents itself is small in comparison.

My challenge to you, the reader, is to reject fear and have faith while knowing and believing that all things work together for good for them who love God, for them who are called according to *his* purpose (Romans 8:28).

## A Poem Pause

"I Told Fear"

I told fear, "You are not welcome in this place." Do you think fear left in haste? No, it stood firm and bold in my face. I told fear, "You are not to enter my heart." Do you think fear fell apart? No, it stood firm and bold in my face. I told fear, "I refuse to give in." Do you think fear dissipated and replied, "Okay. You win"? No, it stood firm and bold in my face, trying to convince me that it was in control. What should I do? And how should I respond to you? A voice spoke loud and clear: *You, my dear, should never fear. You have what it takes to overcome; you have the power to make fear run. The Lord gave his life, for you to live. He already has promised that he will forgive, but our duty is to repent and learn, standing firm in his word and speaking it at every turn. Do you have to fear? The answer is no. But building your faith is the key to letting go. Fear not, my child, for I am with you always. Stand firm and believe for all your days.*

**Fear Memento**

Fear is unbelief in disguise.

## Reflection Moment

Take a moment, sit quietly and still, listen to the voice of the Lord, and take note of what he is speaking to you right now regarding fear. Reflect on past moments, how you responded, and what you can do differently going forward.

### *Reflection Starters*

Has there been a time in my life when I allowed fear to control not only my thoughts but my actions?

When fear presents itself, do I reflect on God's Word and speak to the situation or do I panic and allow fear to dictate my beliefs of what the outcome will be?

_____

_____

_____

_____

_____

_____

_____

_____

_____

_____

## Scripture Moment

"So, you have not received a spirit that makes you fearful slaves. Instead, you received God's Spirit when he adopted you as his own children. Now we call him, 'Abba, Father.'" (Romans 8:15)

"For God has not given us a spirit of fear and timidity, but of power, love, and self-discipline." (2 Timothy 1:7)

# MOMENT OF TRUTH

What is truth? Truth is an individual perception. It is derived from an individual's character, life experiences, filters, and core faith or belief system. Truth drives how an individual views life and life situations. Truth, your truth, determines how you react and respond to situations. What is truth for one may not be truth for another. That is a natural view point of truth.

My moment of truth occurred in the fall of 1991, when I heard the gospel preached and I accepted Christ as my personal savior. Why was that my moment of truth? Because from that very moment, I could see, I mean clearly see, without the blinders of sin on. From that moment, my outlook and view of life changed forever.

I no longer felt inadequate, I no longer desired to die, I no longer felt alone and as if no one loved me. I no longer reacted to situations as though I had no hope. That moment was the very beginning of many moments to come. Some of those moments brought me great joy, but many more moments brought me great sadness.

However, because of that one moment of truth that I had experienced, through hearing and accepting the gospel of Christ, I can endure all faith-defining moments despite the context. I can endure because I have faith in the one true savior who took a moment to carry all my burdens, including the penalty for sin. This allows not only me but you as well to endure the moments he has granted us but to also enjoy them—to be thankful for those moments, to look for and expect more faith-defining moments. For these moments, no matter how they come, are masked opportunities meant to allow us to convene with him.

If you have not yet had your moment of truth, I encourage you to take a moment right now and pray these words: "Lord God, in Jesus's Name, I ask you to forgive me and to cleanse me of my sins. From this day forward, I desire to live each moment of my life in your righteousness, and I thank you for creating in me a clean heart and renewing a right spirit within me. I accept you this moment as my personal savor, and I look forward to the precious moments that we will spend together as I grow in you and my faith. Amen"

## A Poem Pause

"Truth"

My hopes, my dreams, and my desires: these are my truths. My loves, my beliefs, my faith: these are my truths. My emotions, my perspectives, my understandings: these are my truths. What are truths? Truths are what I feel, what touches, what appeals. Truths are what's happening, what's to come, and what's real. Know your truths. Get to know your innermost thoughts, and try not to conceal, for in the truths lies true power to heal.

## Truth Memento

If you are not doing anything in the Lord, not doing anything to further the truth, not doing anything to help and to develop people and their faith, then you are not doing anything at all.

## Reflection Moment

Take a moment, sit quietly and still, listen to the voice of the Lord, and take note of what he is speaking to you right now regarding truth. Reflect on past moments, how you responded, and what you can do differently going forward.

### *Reflection Starters*

Do I allow others to define my truth?

What does truth mean to me?

_____

_____

_____

_____

_____

_____

_____

_____

_____

_____

## Scripture Moment

"For God is Spirit, so those who worship him must worship in spirit and in truth."

(John 4:24)

"And you will know the truth, and the truth will set you free." (John 8:32)

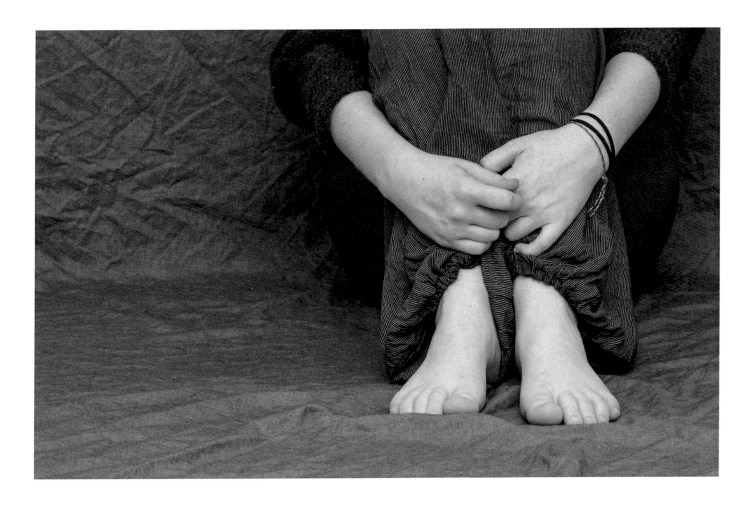

# MOMENT OF DESPAIR

I share one of my moments of despair because it represents my most recent moment. The Lord blessed me with two sons; my eldest has currently lost his way in life and is battling drug addiction and mental illness. This situation has greatly impacted not only my life but the lives of those who love and care about him.

Despite the hurtful moments of watching my first-born struggle in every aspect of human life, from mental anguish to lack of access to normal physical and natural amenities that many of us take for granted, God still speaks words of faith, encouragement, and assurance to me. He told me to lay down my son and give him over to him as a living sacrifice, and he will take care of him. He told me to let go; and that the creator of all things, including me and my son, will deliver. He encouraged me by telling me that when I am having a moment of doubt, a moment of guilt, a moment of grief, to remember his promise. Specifically, he told me to speak this scripture within: "I have never seen the righteous forsaken, nor his seed begging bread" (Psalm 37:25).

The Lord reminded me that our loved ones can be as far from us as possible—in some instances, on the opposite side of the world—and that factor has no bearing on God's ability to protect and deliver! He reminded me that he uses people, places, and things, for he is the great I AM! When I release my son to him, I am expressing my faith and trust in him, which is the key to a stress-free life.

If you have a child or other loved one that has chosen a difficult path in life, I encourage you to let them go. Your role is to step back, trust in and believe that our God is not simply able and willing but that he absolutely will deliver them if we simply believe.

Despair is an emotional feeling of helplessness and hopelessness, with no plan, no way. However, when we look at and dissect the meaning of *despair* based solely on how it makes us feel, the meaning of the word *despair* really does not apply to us. God carried this very emotion to the cross on our behalf so that we no longer must carry this burden. Therefore, in your faith-defining moment of despair, no matter how great or overwhelming the situation may seem, let it go!

Reject despair and use this moment to give thanks to God for delivering you and your loved one from having to engage in such an emotion. I promise you, if you take that moment and instead reflect on God and his word, deliverance will come instantaneously!

As I share this moment, my first-born son has been imprisoned countless times, tried numerous drugs, and been admitted to several psychiatric facilities. He is several states away from me, and has been and may be still homeless. However, I am confident and have great peace knowing that he is in the palms of the great I AM, creator of heaven and earth, and that he couldn't be any safer than he is now. I thank God for my moments of despair, for in them, my faith has grown; my relationship with him is deeper and more profound.

## Despair Memento

Despair is a natural emotion. To embrace it, to foster it, and to accept it is unnatural and leads to even greater despair.

## Reflection Moment

Take a moment, sit quietly and still, listen to the voice of the Lord, and take note of what he is speaking to you right now regarding despair. Reflect on past moments, how you responded, and what you can do differently going forward.

### *Reflection starters*

What brings me the feeling of great despair?

How have I included God during these times?

_____

_____

_____

_____

_____

_____

_____

_____

_____

_____

_____

## Scripture Moment

"We are pressed on every side by troubles, but we are not crushed. We are perplexed, but not driven to despair." (2 Corinthians 4:8)

"You will forget your misery; it will be like water flowing away." (Job 11: 16)

# MOMENT OF JOY

Have you ever experienced true joy? Are you unsure? True joy is an enduring, everlasting, unwavering, and unconditional emotion of pure delight and satisfaction. Despite any circumstance that one may be faced with—no matter what problem presents itself, no matter how complicated the scenario—none of these things affect true joy!

The joy of the Lord is the only true joy. The joy of the Lord has and will continue to be my source of strength. This joy that comes through knowing and accepting the truth that is sourced by God's supernatural characteristics and fueled by faith in him. In my life, and even at this present moment, I am faced with situations that are unpleasant, overwhelming, and undesirable; however, I face them with true joy! I am excited because I have joy in knowing that all things are temporary. I am excited because I know that there is a solution to every problem. I am excited because all things are working together for my good. I am excited because no weapon formed against me shall prosper. I am excited and full of joy because I know that I am the righteousness of God through Christ Jesus. I am excited, and my joy is unwavering, because I know that my Lord will allow no more to come upon me than I shall be able to bear; but he will make a way of escape that I may be able to bear it!

You see, he has already made that way of escape for us when he sent his son Jesus to die on the cross for our sins. That was the escape: when he rose from the dead and went back to the heavens and sat at the right hand of God the Father. That was the way made that we could bare all things. God sent us his spirit, in the form of the Holy Ghost, and if you receive it, you can bear it!

True joy is not easily understood by those who have not yet received the true joy maker and who do not yet believe that true joy exists. True joy is not acceptable to the natural eye or natural way of thinking, it's a faith thing, it's a supernatural thing that more than surpasses the natural adversity, and it omits it all together, making whatever the situation insignificant and void of influence.

Why wouldn't you want true joy? Why would anyone reject such a gift? When you experience true joy, it's a moment to reassure. It's a moment that is enduring and encouraging. To go through this life without it is a great tragedy. If you have not experienced true joy, I encourage you to take a moment to seek God and to accept his promise of true joy. It gives me great joy to share this message. It gives me great joy to know that you have received it, and it gives me great joy to know that all current, past, and future trials of life have no adverse effect on me or you because we have received true joy!

**Joy Memento**

True joy to some may seem unobtainable; to those who believe this, it is.

## Reflection Moment

Take a moment, sit quietly and still, listen to the voice of the Lord, and take note of what he is speaking to you right now regarding joy. Reflect on past moments, how you responded, and what you can do differently going forward.

### Reflection Starters

What brings me great joy?

When faced with trials and tribulations, do I reflect on the joy of the Lord?

_____

_____

_____

_____

_____

_____

_____

_____

_____

_____

## Scripture Moment

"But let all who take refuge in you rejoice; let them sing joyful praises forever. Spread your protection over them, that all who love your name may be filled with joy." (Psalm 5:11)

"The seed on the rocky soil represents those who hear the message and immediately receive it with joy." (Mark 4:16)

# MOMENT OF STRENGTH

There are moments in our lives when we are forced to be strong. Many of us have been told, "Be strong." I admit that I have asked myself, "How?" How am I to be strong when I have no strength? I have found that, separate from my faith, I cannot be strong within myself. True strength only comes through faith, and Jesus is the source of my faith and, therefore, my strength.

My upbringing was the training ground for my life. It was the foundation that was designed to build my character and outlook on life. This is true for everyone; therefore, it is important for parents to know that our upbringing, the way we, as children, are raised, treated, and talked to, matters. These young experiences serve as the fuel, which feeds our characters and the way we think, perceive, and ultimately respond and react to life situations.

If we, as parents, remember this, we will take great care in how we interact with our children and how we shape their environments. We will ensure that their experiences are those that attribute to characteristics of strength, loyalty, integrity, and empathy for others.

I grew up in a low-income housing project, the oldest of four daughters, each with a different father. Mine was murdered when I was just five years old, leaving a reputation that requires me to be very discrete in revealing who my father is. This has positioned me to turn to the one and only true source of strength. Through faith, we can endure all things. Through faith, we can overcome the most seemingly unbearable circumstances. However, without faith, we are but mere humans, weak to all things, having no strength. We could crumble at the very sign of distress. It is important to utilize faith as you would a muscle, for the more you exercise your faith, the stronger it becomes.

When life presents what looks like a giant of a problem, it will not be a match for your faith! Be strong in the Lord and you can go through this life carefree and full of optimistic energy. You can encourage others along the way to join your marathon, your strength-building and faith-building journey.

There will be times when you do not feel strong. There will be times when you feel like giving up. Remember that you become strong through a process; over time your strength builds upon itself. When you are tempted to be weak, reject weakness and call for strength. For when you are in your most unbearable and vulnerable moment, that is when you are the strongest.

I am reminded of Jesus dying on the cross; he exposed some signs of vulnerability when he called out to God the Father; however, he did not give into that emotion. He mustered through it and gave up the Ghost! He is our most perfect example of strength. Exercise your faith muscle. Speak to whatever situation presents itself that is unpleasant to you, and call what you want that situation to be, despite how it looks. When you do this, you exhibit strength through faith, and your situation must change because it will obey what you have spoken out of your mouth.

Remember that God's Word, his promises, and his plans are all strength-builders. When we stay in his will, succumb to his plan, and take the actions directed by him, we are strong.

## Strength Memento

Strength and faith are companions for endurance.

## Reflection Moment

Take a moment, sit quietly and still, listen to the voice of the Lord, and take note of what he is speaking to you right now regarding strength. Reflect on past moments, how you responded, and what you can do differently going forward.

### *Reflection Starters*

What or who is my source of strength?

Do I rely too much on myself and others in the time of need?

_____

_____

_____

_____

_____

_____

_____

_____

_____

_____

_____

## Scripture Moment

"The LORD is my rock, my fortress, and my savior; my God is my rock, in whom I find protection. He is my shield, the power that saves me, and my place of safety." (Psalm 18:2)

"For I can do everything through Christ, who gives me strength." (Philippians 4:13)

# MOMENT OF LOVE

Despite what most people believe what love is, it is an action. Love is something that you do; it is represented beyond simply saying I love you. Loving someone or something is backed up by the action! Test this perspective and reflect on John 3:16: "God so loved the world that he gave his only begotten son, that whosoever believeth in him should not perish, but have everlasting life."

The operable word in this scripture is *gave*. God did something to show that he loved us! God proved his love for you and for me when he sent his son as a living sacrifice to die on the cross on our behalf, carrying our sin debt. There could be no greater proof of love than dying because of it, for it, and on its behalf! When I reflect upon love, it prompts me to give. When I reflect upon love, it prompts me to do. When I reflect upon love, it prompts me to act!

Love will compel you to go out of your way for others. It will cause you to position yourself to put others first. It will cause you to be on the giving end of the spectrum. From this end of the spectrum, the giving end, the doing end, the action-oriented end, you are forever able to receive love in return. I prayed, "Lord bless me to be a blessing!" Then I was in a position where I was constantly doing, constantly being called upon, constantly being asked of, constantly being called to action. I said, "Wait a minute. People are only reaching out to me when they are in need."

The Lord quickly reminded me, "You asked me to bless you to be a blessing, and you are able to bless, to help others, and to demonstrate to them how much you love them. Why, then, are you questioning and complaining about the call to action?" I quickly repented! I set out to love others on purpose. Despite how they treat me, I love anyway.

Those closest to me often ask, "Why do you even bother?" They say, "I would not put up with that." They say, "People are not deserving of you." I often smile and say, "I'd much rather be the one being hurt versus the one causing the hurt. I'd much rather be the giver than the receiver or the one giving the help versus needing the help!"

I continually seek out ways to prove my love for others. Have you ever heard the saying, "I can show you better than I can tell you?" That is one of my mottos in life! I'd much rather show than tell, for the profound and undeniable proof of how one feels is in one's actions! One will never be without, one will never have to want, and one will never be on the losing end if one chooses to simply love.

When you are oppressed by a situation or a person, choose love. When you are tempted to be offended, choose love. When you are slighted and mistreated, choose love. For in return, love will be bestowed upon you, and you will heap coals of fire upon the heads of those who choose the contrary.

Great love has God bestowed upon us. Who are we that we should not demonstrate and show love? God's love is unconditional. We did nothing and can do nothing to deserve his love. He simply chose to love us. Why wouldn't we choose to love others? You might be thinking, *But they do not deserve my love!* That's irrelevant. You will be judged for your choice to love, and they will be judged for the actions that cause us to feel that they do not deserve our love. Remember, our actions did not stop God from loving us. It did not stop him from designing a plan of salvation for us, and even today, despite how we act, what we do, and what we say, it does not stop him from loving us even now. Take a moment to love in deed, for to do so exhibits the loving characteristics our Lord and Savior exhibited when he so loved the world.

## A Poem Pause

"The Simplicity of Love"

Love, just four letters that mean so much

Love can come in many forms, including a touch

Love, an actionable word, so often referred to

Love, with deep meaning and substance, if applied through and through

Love, who has the ability to do this word justice?

Love, those who serve the highest and who he has entrusted

Love, it knows no wrong; it holds no grudges

Love, its repeatable; its sustainable; it never judges

**Love Memento**

The substitute for love is nonexistent. Unconditional love loves despite the return on investment.

## Reflection Moment

Take a moment, sit quietly and still, listen to the voice of the Lord, and take note of what he is speaking to you right now regarding love. Reflect on past moments, how you responded, and what you can do differently going forward.

### *Reflection Starters*

Am I loving in word and in deed?

How do I demonstrate love to myself and to others?

_____

_____

_____

_____

_____

_____

_____

_____

_____

_____

## Scripture Moment

"For you bless the godly, O LORD; you surround them with your shield of love." (Psalm 5:12)

"So now I am giving you a new commandment: Love each other. Just as I have loved you, you should love each other." (John 13:34)

# MOMENT OF REJECTION

Rejection is the opposite of acceptance, and it can have an everlasting effect. However, what if I told you that rejection is also something that can be overcome? It too can be rejected. Rejection is an act that is taken by an individual or a group of individuals. This act of rejection is a choice made by those who choose to accept a person or situation. Those individuals have made a conscious decision to refuse to embrace, accept, or engage in a situation or with an individual. These individuals made the choice to reject and therefore own that conscious decision.

If you have ever been on the receiving end of rejection, you are the intended recipient and receiver. I am here to tell you that you too have a choice! You can choose to accept or to receive the rejection.

Or you can reject rejection! You might be asking yourself, "How can I reject rejection?" The answer is simple: Refuse to receive it! How? Do not give into the behaviors and characteristics that are exhibited from a recipient of rejection. *What does that look like?* you may be wondering. You love, show kindness, show grace, show mercy, and show forgiveness, even though rejection has presented itself. You ignore and resist rejection not simply in word but in deed. You resist the temptation to behave as a victim of rejection; you decide not to give rejection authority and power over you, your actions, and your thoughts.

You may still be pondering the questions of why and how? The *why* to this simplistic mystery of life is the key to the *how*. The *why* behind rejecting rejection is because Jesus came into the world to save the world from sin and the punishment that comes with sin. He was flat-out rejected! He even first came into his own lineage, his own blood line, and was flat-out rejected! Suppose he had accepted and received rejection? Suppose he had become a victim of rejection? We would have had no hope; we would be doomed for hell without a chance of redemption.

Jesus rejected rejection. He went into the uttermost parts of the earth, spreading the truth, touching lives, warning, admonishing, and encouraging people to accept him as their personal savior. Guess what? Some eventually accepted him and some rejected him, but to those who accepted him, he gave them the power to become the sons of God! That very act of acceptance leads to the *how*. How can we reject rejection? We must first accept Jesus, put aside rejection, and believe in the one and only true Christ, for when we do, we accept the power to reject rejection. From there, we will have the divine ability to overcome rejection and all the baggage that comes with it! Thoughts of suicide, thoughts of doom and gloom, feelings of insecurity, lack of confidence, thoughts and feelings of emptiness and loneliness, feeling as though no one cares, feeling as though you are null and void—these descriptors are the baggage that come with being a victim of rejection. Most of my childhood and early adulthood, I was a victim of rejection. I carried this baggage with me into my marriage, into motherhood, into friendships, and right on into my relationship with the Lord. It was right there in that relationship with Christ where I learned that to accept rejection is a choice. It was there that I learned that just because rejection presents itself does not mean I must accept it. I learned to resist rejection by being kind on purpose. I learned to exhibit the opposite characteristics of the victimlike characteristics that were trying so very hard to impose themselves upon me.

From this learning, practiced over time and put into action, I became free of that rejected mentality. Rejection no longer has a stronghold over me, although there are moments when I am tempted to feel and accept rejection. I resist those feelings, and I hold to a promise that I made to myself: I shall never be the victim again but shall forever be the victor! I realized and hope that you know and understand that the devil is out to steal, kill, and destroy. He has many cunning tricks to help him accomplish this. Satan knows that if he can get in your mind and if he can convince you to accept rejection, and therefore all the baggage that comes along with it, he will be well on his way to robbing you of all the wonderful blessings that God has in store just for you.

I pray that in the moment when rejection presents itself, you take a moment to reflect and remind yourself that you are the victor and not the victim. Reject rejection in that very moment and it shall flee!

**Rejection Memento**

The act of rejection is seeded and rooted with a cunning and evil plot; however, the act of rejecting rejection has the power to deplete, destroy, and supersede its ultimate plan.

## Reflection Moment

Take a moment, sit quietly and still, listen to the voice of the Lord, and take note of what he is speaking to you right now regarding rejection. Reflect on past moments, how you responded, and what you can do differently going forward.

### *Reflection Starters*

Have I ever felt rejected? What did I do? How did I respond?

Have I ever acted in a way that left someone else feeling rejected?

_____

_____

_____

_____

_____

_____

_____

_____

_____

_____

## Scripture Moment

"Rebellion is as sinful as witchcraft, and stubbornness as bad as worshiping idols. So because you have rejected the command of the LORD, he has rejected you as king." (1 Samuel 15:23)

"Then Jesus asked them, "Didn't you ever read this in the Scriptures? "The stone that the builders rejected has now become the cornerstone. This is the Lord's doing, and it is wonderful to see." (Matthew 21:42)

## MOMENT OF HAPPINESS

Happiness comes from within. I can attest that true happiness is purely unconditional, meaning that although you may be impacted by current circumstances, the situation has no effect on your happiness.

I can recall early in my life when I was so very unhappy, I allowed every situation, every life event, to have a profound impact on my emotional state, on my outlook. Often I reacted to temporary situations with very permanent thoughts. I am grateful that through coming to know Jesus as my personal savior,

I came to recognize and experience happiness. I can recall being forced to leave my mother's home at a young age, pregnant and married at a very young age, with minimal to no income.

I can recall the struggle and the challenging relationship I had with my mother and how I allowed all those things to impact my happiness. I had moments and thoughts of suicide, thinking I would never experience happiness.

Today, I reflect on those situations, and I am so grateful for each of them. I would not change any of those experiences if I could. Why? Because those situations, those moments, led me to sustain a close relationship with God, who took me in the palm of his hands, groomed me, protected me, and encouraged me to look to him, the author and the finisher of my faith. I can truly and honestly assert that I am happy. Regardless of what I face, regardless of what I have faced, regardless of what I will face, I am happy.

Happiness is a choice, and we have been given the freedom of choice. When we are sad, we believe it is because of the situation; however, it is because of the choice we made to be sad about a situation. Sometimes it's a conscious choice, and other times it is an unconscious choice. However, we own the responsibility for our choices, and therefore, we own the experiences that we endure as we journey through this life.

I can attest that one will never experience true happiness until one has accepted and bonded with Jesus. Happiness, his happiness, cannot be experienced separate from him. The world has a perception that happiness comes with wealth, with having material things, or with being in control and in a position of power. I can tell you with absolute confidence that you can have these things and never experience happiness.

If you doubt this perspective, simply look at those in positions of power. Look at those who have great wealth, study the tragedies of their lives, and assess if what they endured prior to their tragic ends reflected happiness. If someone asked me to describe what it means to be happy, I would respond, "Happiness is the state of being free from sin and being committed to having faith in God." Imagine this: the one true being who is in control of everything and all things—who, at his voice, even death obeys. He says to you, "I forgive you of your sins. You can have all things according to my riches and glory. I love you unconditionally. That type of happiness can endure all things because of its source.

I encourage you to look beyond yourself for happiness. Take a moment to reflect on the source of happiness. Let go of the world's thought patterns and traditional outlook, and challenge yourself to accept and acknowledge the one who is the giver of true happiness.

My very first encounter of this type of happiness came more than twenty years ago. I recall answering the altar call and being baptized and giving praise to God for his great deliverance. Wow, what a feeling! If you are one who is walking in happiness, others will gravitate toward you. They will want to be around you. They will not know why, but it is because of your source of happiness. That source of happiness exudes freedom, compassion, love, and all those godly characteristics that draw people toward righteousness.

I am so very grateful that the Lord saw fit and continues to allow me to experience moments of happiness, for in these moments, I find relief and peace.

## Happiness Memento

Happiness and peace are connected, and their bonds are unbreakable. You can't have one without the other.

## Reflection Moment

Take a moment, sit quietly and still, listen to the voice of the Lord, and take note of what he is speaking to you right now regarding happiness. Reflect on past moments, how you responded and what you can do differently going forward.

### Reflection Starters

Do I create experiences and situations that brings happiness to others?

If not, what's preventing me from doing so?

_____

_____

_____

_____

_____

_____

_____

_____

_____

_____

## Scripture Moment

"You will enjoy the fruit of your labor. How joyful and prosperous you will be!" (Psalm 128:2)

"But even if you suffer for doing what is right, God will reward you for it. So don't worry or be afraid of their threats." (1 Peter 3:14)

# MOMENT OF FRUSTRATION

Frustration, like other emotions and reactions, is a choice. We have free will to receive and accept the spirit of frustration. When you are faced with a situation that you have no control over and the outcome is not meeting your expectations, frustration presents itself. How do you recognize frustration? How do you reject frustration? How do you overcome it? Frustration is the origin of a lack of self-control and, to some degree, a lack of faith and belief. Yes, we are all guilty of falling victim to the spirit of frustration. In fact, as I am writing at this very moment, I am repenting for having fallen victim to acting out of frustration.

How do we recognize this ugly phenomenon? In the heat of a faith-defining moment or experience, you act in a way or say things that you would have refrained from if you were not overwhelmed with the feeling of frustration. People have taken lives, even their very own lives, due to frustration. You can recognize a frustrated moment by taking a minute to evaluate and check your emotions. In many situations, pausing is the best practice; often, our third thought is our best. Think about the thoughts that are coming to mind and simply reject the ugly ones by replacing them with thoughts that are pleasant, positive, and abundantly productive. Rationalize with yourself first before trying to rationalize with others.

Another tip to overcome a moment of frustration is to exercise your faith. If a situation has occurred that is or has caused you to feel frustrated, recall the one whom you serve! Reflect on his promises. One of my favorite scriptures is one I often lean on when tempted to feel frustrated: "But in that coming day no weapon turned against you will succeed. You will silence every voice raised up to accuse you. These benefits are enjoyed by the servants of the LORD; their vindication will come from me. I, the LORD, have spoken" (Isaiah 54:17). I believe that this scripture is applicable in any situation that we could ever be faced with in this life.

I am convinced the key to success in any situation is to simply believe and to have faith in God! Trust that even in this faith-defining moment, whatever that moment may be, he has your best interest at heart. You may have thought that the outcome should have been A, but his plan all along was for it to be Z. Trust that he knows what is best for you.

When we accept frustration, when we act out of frustration, we are saying, "God, give me the wheel. I can direct my own path, and I am all knowing." These actions do not reflect faith; these actions do not reflect trust. Therefore, they often lead to permanent and irreversible actions made from frustration based upon a temporary situation.

If you are guilty of reacting in the moment, do not feel condemned, but take these words under advisement, practice these tips in your next moment of frustration, and experience what freedom really is.

## Frustration Memento

Frustration is a matter of reaction in the heat of a moment. Trust and faith in God are matters that deliver in every moment and every time.

# Reflection Moment

Take a moment, sit quietly and still, listen to the voice of the Lord, and take note of what he is speaking to you right now regarding frustration. Reflect on past moments, how you responded, and what you can do differently going forward.

## *Reflection Starters*

What types of events trigger the feeling of frustration?

When the spirit of frustration is present, what can I do to counter that emotion?

_____

_____

_____

_____

_____

_____

_____

_____

_____

_____

## Scripture Moment

"Don't be afraid, for I am with you. Don't be discouraged, for I am your God. I will strengthen you and help you. I will hold you up with my victorious right hand." (Isaiah 41:10)

"Give all your worries and cares to God, for he cares about you." (1 Peter 5:7)

# MOMENT OF VICTORY

The words *victory* and *overcome* are one and the same. If the word *overcome* is indeed an accurate description of the word *victory*, which I believe it is, then we can all consider ourselves victorious overcomers!

When we accepted Jesus as our Savior, he declared us victorious, and this is true because he is victorious! He overcame the world, sickness, sin, and death. He conquered all that was put before him because of his power and faith in God's plan. When we made the choice to follow Jesus, we chose victory over defeat! We are overcomers because Jesus overcame.

We experience moments of victory every day and at every moment. When we breathe, when we rise in the morning, when we lay down at night, when we travel throughout the day and arrive safely we experience victory. When we maintain our relationship with our Lord, when we acknowledge him, when we acknowledge others, when we show acts of love and kindness instead of acts of bitterness and deceit, we experience victory. When we resist the temptation to give up, to give in, to fret, to doubt, to fear, to hate, we are experiencing victory!

I recall one of many victorious moments, and that is when my family and I were faced with financial struggles. The mortgage was behind two to three months. The gas utility was cut off due to inability to pay. Telephone service was disconnected due to inability to pay. We had no money for food and just barely enough money to purchase fuel for our cars to make it to and from work. It was indeed a dark, faith-defining moment.

However, my moment of victory was not only the result but was how I endured and how I responded within those dark moments. I decided to call what I wanted. I literally spoke out of my mouth phrases such as, "Money cometh to me now," "Situation change in Jesus name," "I come against lack and poverty in the name of Jesus," etc. By standing on God's promises, by believing that this too shall pass, and by calling victory, guess what? Victory came!

God showed up and made a way of escape that had nothing to do with borrowing money. His divine plans and interventions are creative and innovative. Our minds can't fathom the solutions that he has for us and for our situations.

That faith-defining moment in my life was an amazing experience that serves as a faith foundation for me even to this day. When I am tempted to feel, act, or think in a less than victorious way, I recall that moment, and I am encouraged. After that moment in my life, the Lord spoke these words to me: He said, "Rhoda, I will always do this for you if you simply allow me to." These words sound so simple. What we struggle with as humans is giving over control. We must give it all over to God because he is the only one who can fully deliver. He is the creator of heaven and earth, including the creator of us, so we must trust and not doubt.

I will forever hold these words dear and near to my heart. There is really no reason at all to ever doubt, fret, or fear when we know him. He declared us victorious from the beginning when he sacrificed his son, Jesus, who died for our sins and rose for our justification. Remember this: no matter what moment presents itself or what presents itself within any moment, if what you are faced with is not perfectly aligned with the promises that God left on record for you, then you do not have to accept it! You can rejoice in any situation knowing that you are victorious and that you are an overcomer of a very temporary situation. For that moment is meant to build your faith story so that you can help others to build theirs.

## Victory Memento

Victory is only attained and sustained through the power of God.

## Reflection Moment

Take a moment, sit quietly and still, listen to the voice of the Lord, and take note of what he is speaking to you right now regarding victory. Reflect on past moments, how you responded, and what you can do differently going forward.

### Reflection Starters

Do I conduct myself as a victor or a victim?

What behaviors do I display that exude the characteristics of a victorious warrior?

_____

_____

_____

_____

_____

_____

_____

_____

_____

_____

## Scripture Moment

"But thank God! He gives us victory over sin and death through our Lord Jesus Christ." (1 Corinthians 15:57)

"For every child of God defeats this evil world, and we achieve this victory through our faith." (1 John 5:4)

# MOMENT OF CONFIDENCE

We can only be certain when we have Jesus on our side and, therefore, in our lives. Individuals who have confidence but lack a relationship with Christ are uncertain in all their ways.

Confidence is often mistaken as arrogance, and arrogance is often mistaken as confidence. How does one distinguish between the two? A person who is confident practices faith in God knowing that there is no failure in him (God). A person who is arrogant lacks a true understanding of faith and what it means to rely on God versus relying on self. People like this only believe in themselves and their abilities. To walk in arrogance is dangerous. Not only do we, as humans, have no ability of our own as we are totally and wholly reliant upon God, but when we walk in arrogance, we are sending a message to God saying, "I got this. I can do it better, and I am in control." The fact of the matter is that we are never, ever in control. The only control we have is the control to choose. We can choose to believe and accept God, or we can choose not to believe God or even to believe that he even exists.

To have confidence in ourselves is unintelligent. As humans, we can fail. God, as the Supreme Being, cannot. One who puts his faith and confidence in God has just embarked upon wisdom. Jesus is pleased with confidence as it symbolizes that one has faith. Uphold your faith in God's word, and you can live a confident life knowing that no weapon formed against you shall prosper, all things are working together for your good, and Jesus has your back always!

I recall a point in time that was very trying and stressful. I had no money to meet current or future needs, yet I was 100 percent confident that the Lord would change my situation. He spoke to me during that time, saying, "Rhoda, your situation has to change because it is contradicting what my word says." After listening to the voice of the Lord and refocusing my attention on him and his word instead of focusing on and giving all attention and energy to my current situation, my faith in God and his word soared. And guess what? It didn't take long for God to come through! I received a great financial breakthrough that allowed us to not only meet our needs but to meet the needs of others.

If you have moments when you lack confidence, I encourage you to go to the word. Shift your focus, speak what you want, give attention and energy to those things that will cause your situation to change, and confidence will come through faith. Faith will bring about blessings. Blessings will bring about joy. Joy will bring about strength, and strength will bring about endurance.

## Confidence Memento

A confident man is a man of faith. An arrogant man is a man of unbelief.

## Reflection Moment

Take a moment, sit quietly and still, listen to the voice of the Lord, and take note of what he is speaking to you right now regarding confidence. Reflect on past moments, how you responded, and what you can do differently going forward.

### Reflection Starters

Do I exude confidence? If so, in what ways?

If not, what can I do differently to present myself in a more confident manner?

_____

_____

_____

_____

_____

_____

_____

_____

_____

_____

_____

_____

## Scripture Moment

"It is better to take refuge in the LORD than to trust in people." (Psalm 118:8)

"For the LORD is your security. He will keep your foot from being caught in a trap." (Proverbs 3:26)

# MOMENT OF INSPIRATION

Have you ever been inspired? To inspire is to ignite a desire. We, as human beings and as children of God, are inspired daily. We have influence to ignite positivity, and unfortunately, we have influence to ignite the opposite. However, by the grace of God, most of us are inspired for the good. Many of us inspire others to do well, to make productive and positive choices.

Reflect upon a loved one, a friend, or just simply someone you had a very brief interaction with. Did you inspire them? I believe that every human interaction that we have is an opportunity to inspire. Inspiration is a God-given attribute that we all have. This is the one gift that we can choose to give freely. But the one universal gift to uplift, to encourage, to motivate, and to inspire is not as commonly given as it should be. Why is that the case? It is a natural habit to focus inwardly only on one's self, and when we do this, we are literally blind to the needs, emotions, and experiences of others. Suppose Jesus was self-centered. Suppose when he entered earth as the Son of God, he focused solely on himself. Suppose he ignored the moments and the opportunities to positively inspire. We would be doomed—an uninspired people, lost without hope.

Hope. Yes, that is what inspiration is all about: inspiring hope into the spirit and psyche of another human being. What a profound moment and opportunity! I have had the fortune to reside on both ends of the inspiration spectrum. I have been inspired, and I have inspired. I was inspired to accept Jesus as my personal savior! Someone cared enough about me to share the good news of salvation with me, which inspired me to repent, to cast away my worldly ways, and to build a relationship with God the Father. From that paramount moment of inspiration, many doors opened, leading to deeper and further inspiring moments in my life.

I, like many others, have been faced with several faith-trying situations. A dying mother is a very tough moment—watching your mother die of cancer right before your eyes; however, I am inspired. A mentally ill son is a very hurtful and almost surreal experience—to witness your firstborn being used by demonic spirits and turn to drugs to cope versus turning to Jesus for hope. Yet, I am inspired.

I had a very trying battle with my lifelong fight with obesity and dealt with the stigma that comes with being overweight. I was forced to compensate by overachieving in other areas of my life, including a deep desire to have people, friends, and family who care for and love me for who I am. Yet I am inspired. I am the daughter of a known hitman, with knowledge of people he has murdered, and have met some of the people his actions impacted. Yet I am inspired. I almost drowned at the age of fourteen, was hit by a car at the age of ten, and had a bout with renal failure due to an allergic reaction to medication and almost died. Yet I am inspired. I was inspired to write this book in the format that it is in and to share fragments of my personal struggles only to inspire others who, in this life, have experienced the very same faith-defining moments that I have.

Our challenge is not only to inspire but to accept inspiration, for it refuels us and allows us to continue to inspire others. To give and to receive inspiration is to give and to receive hope, freedom, joy, and deliverance. When we accept Jesus as our personal Savior, we are inspired by the power of God, and we are empowered to inspire others.

## Inspiration Memento

Go inspire, for an uninspired person is consumed and destroyed by despair.

## Reflection Moment

Take a moment, sit quietly and still, listen to the voice of the Lord, and take note of what he is speaking to you right now regarding inspiration. Reflect on past moments, how you responded, and what you can do differently going forward.

### *Reflection Starters*

What inspires me?

Do I intentionally inspire others? If so, how?

_____

_____

_____

_____

_____

_____

_____

_____

_____

_____

## Scripture Moment

"But there is a spirit within people, the breath of the Almighty within them, that makes them intelligent." (Job 32:8)

"All Scripture is inspired by God and is useful to teach us what is true and to make us realize what is wrong in our lives. It corrects us when we are wrong and teaches us to do what is right." (2 Timothy 3:16)

# MOMENT OF GRIEF AND SORROW

Have you ever lost a loved one? I have often been told there is nothing like losing a child or a mother. I have experienced both.

When our loved ones pass on from this life to the next, it is often a painful experience for those of us who are left to grieve their passing. We long for their presence, their voices, their scents, and their smiles; however, we are left with only memories. Until I lost my mother, I had never experienced that level of grief and sorrow. It is a level of grief that is unexplainable, yet I continuously attempt to put how I feel into words. I describe this grief as a feeling of loneliness, an abrupt removal of the invisible umbilical cord that you never even realized was there until your mother is gone.

To lose a mother—what a blow! I recall thinking to myself, *No one should ever have to experience this loss, and it hurts so deeply.* And to have lost her so soon, the age of sixty-two years. It just does not seem like she lived a full life. Grief and sorrow, once experienced, are emotions that remain with us forever. These emotions never really leave. They don't fade over time; they don't become minimized. Once experienced, these emotions are everlasting. They become a part of who you are. However, with time and over time, we learn to cope and to manage these emotions. Having watched my mother make the transition, although hurtful, there were many moments of joy, even during those trying times. In her final moments, she accepted Christ, she laughed, she caused laughter. We sang songs, and we held hands. I recall one moment when she was very alert and conscious, I read a scripture to her, and at the end of the reading, I said, "Where you are going, when you get there, even if you had a choice, you would never choose to come back to this place."

She responded ever so gently and sweetly, "Not ever," and we exchanged smiles.

You see, even in moments of grief and sorrow, there are opportunities to rejoice. Even in moments like the ones I describe, we have choices. We choose how we are going to deal with the grief and sorrow, we choose how we are going to deal with the loss of a loved one, and we choose how we are going to react and respond in any given situation. Life is all about choices: to live a life full of hurt, sorrow, and grief. Allowing these emotions to dominate and control our actions, reactions and behaviors is not wise. In fact, to allow oneself to be overcome with grief and sorrow for an extended period is risky.

It is perfectly fine to take a moment to grieve. In fact, it is natural to do so; however, only allow grief to persist in designated moments. Choose to allow joy, happiness, positivity, and encouragement to dominate in your life, especially when dealing with the loss of a loved one. I have found that choosing to focus on the positives in all circumstances is way more fulfilling, uplifting, and natural than focusing on the negatives. In the case of my mother, she is no longer suffering; we are no longer suffering by watching her suffer. My mother is now in the presence of her creator, singing praises of joy!

I will never forget what she whispered to me just forty-eight hours before she took her final breath. She said, "They didn't want me yet. My robe was not ready." I was overcome with relief and great joy to hear these words, "My robe was not ready yet." Reflect on these words. Wow! A robe was being prepared for her. Now that is something to rejoice about. My mother was having a robe of righteousness prepared specifically for her!

April 5, 2015, Easter Sunday, at 11:09 a.m., her robe was made ready, and she departed this life. I received those final moments and the last moment as reassurance that she is okay and she is now resting from her labor. Do I miss Dorothy, my mother? Yes, deeply, but I choose to not allow grief and sorrow to dominate my being. I put these emotions in their place. I have chosen joy, happiness, gladness, and sweet memories as companions to get me through each day, and you know what? So far, this choice has proven to be one of the wisest I have made to date.

## Grief and Sorrow Memento

Grief and sorrow are cousins, holding hands, but joy and peace are present
and available to help you to withstand. Choose your companions.

## Reflection Moment

Take a moment, sit quietly and still, listen to the voice of the Lord, and take note of what he is speaking to you right now regarding grief and sorrow. Reflect on past moments, how you responded, and what you can do differently going forward.

### *Reflection Starters*

Have I truly grieved over the loss of my loved one?

What are some ways that I can relieve myself from the feelings of grief and sorrow?

_____

_____

_____

_____

_____

_____

_____

_____

_____

## Scripture Moment

"Obey your spiritual leaders, and do what they say. Their work is to watch over your souls, and they are accountable to God. Give them reason to do this with joy and not with sorrow. That would certainly not be for your benefit." (Hebrews 13:17)

"So you have sorrow now, but I will see you again; then you will rejoice, and no one can rob you of that joy." (John 16:22)

# MOMENT OF ENCOURAGEMENT

Be encouraged and of good faith. What rings true is the voice of many saying, "This is easier said than done!" Did you know that speaking words out of your mouth yields the desire, drive, and faith to set things into action?

We have all been in situations where we could have benefited from a word or two of encouragement. It is impossible to live in this world without one another; we need each other for support and encouragement, as we are social beings. When we lose a loved one, when we face a bad break up, when we lose a job, when we are experiencing financial struggles, when we are having health issues, when we are feeling alone, when we make bad decisions, those critical and often delicate moments in our lives require encouragement.

It is fulfilling for me to be available, fully present, and more than willing to encourage. In fact, there are few things that give me more joy than the opportunity to encourage someone else. Why is that? Because as I build up another person, as I remind them of their blessings, as I challenge them to change their perspective and viewpoint about their situation, I forget all about myself and my problems. I am, in that moment, totally and whole-heartedly focused on encouraging that person who is before me. This is an opportunity, in and of itself, to seize the moment, to lift that person up, to offer potentially life-altering words of encouragement, and to leave them with a lasting impression that they can get through any moment!

As we are placed in situations where a loved one, a friend, or a casual associate willingly opens and begins to share, we are to take advantage of those moments and remind that person of all the good things that exist in his or her life. We are to refocus that person, encourage him or her to reflect on all the many blessings that exist, help that person see the positives instead of focusing on the negatives. I would venture to say in most cases, those individuals will eventually see that their good days outweigh their bad days. They will remember that all things are temporary and that whatever they are faced with at that moment will eventually pass. For every problem, there is a solution.

It does not take a whole lot of time or a whole lot of words to encourage. You can encourage with a smile, by acknowledging a person, by giving them a compliment, or by simply saying hello. There are times when we ourselves are going through trials and tribulations, and we are so down that we can't see up. This, my friend, is the best way to build yourself up: by building up and encouraging someone else.

It is natural for us to experience discouragement, but it is also natural for us to offer encouragement. Notice that there is another word embedded in the word *encouragement*, and that is the word *courage*. It takes courage to step outside of yourself and your own personal circumstances to offer up encouragement. Unbeknownst to many, it is an act of faith. By faith, you believe that the Holy Spirit will give you the words that will penetrate and aid the person in need. And by faith, you trust that the person in need will receive.

I can recall several moments in my life when I needed encouragement, and I can recall that very often, there was no one willing to offer me the encouragement that I needed and longed for. Then I remembered Jesus, my Lord and my Savior. He speaks quietly and reminds me constantly that he will never leave me and that he is always present. The same is true for you. Jesus loves you so very much that it grieves him to see you discouraged. He died on the cross and rose from the dead that you may be encouraged! No matter what you are going through, no matter what you face in life, no matter how big and ugly it looks, God is greater!

Be encouraged, stay encouraged, and go encourage others. For to do so is the act of seed-sowing, for which you will reap in due season if you faint not.

## Encouragement Memento

Encouraging others is the secret to encouraging one's own self.

## Reflection Moment

Take a moment, sit quietly and still, listen to the voice of the Lord, and take note of what he is speaking to you right now regarding encouragement. Reflect on past moments, how you responded, and what you can do differently going forward.

### Reflection Starters

Have I encouraged someone lately?

How do I remain encouraged?

_____

_____

_____

_____

_____

_____

_____

_____

_____

_____

## Scripture Moment

"I weep with sorrow; encourage me by your word." (Psalm 119:28)

"David was now in great danger because all his men were very bitter about losing their sons and daughters, and they began to talk of stoning him. But David found strength in the LORD his God." (1 Samuel 30:6)

## MOMENT OF GRACE AND MERCY

In my forty-plus years, I have had six *known* near-death experiences! At the young age of five years old, I witnessed a young lady being murdered by gun fire. At the age of ten years old, I was hit by a hit-and-run driver. At the age of 14 years old I nearly drowned and was pulled from the water by a life guard just in the moment when I had given up. At the age of 16 years old I was in a car accident, hit by a driver at full speed who was driving down a one way street the wrong way, totaled the car. At the age of twenty years old and pregnant, I nearly died from toxemia. And in 2008, I suffered from renal failure due to an allergic reaction to medication that went undiscovered for several weeks, causing my body to nearly enter shock from toxicities.

I share these facts to illuminate God's grace and mercy! I am certain many have had near-death experiences, and I am even more certain that I have had more that I am even aware of! I recall when I was ill in 2008, sick for several weeks, literally dying, the Lord spoke these words to me: "I am the core of your existence. In me you live, and you move, and you have your being." I will never forget those moments when I sat wondering what was wrong with me and why the doctors did not care enough to probe. The Lord would consistently whisper those words to me. Only after entering the hospital and finally being diagnosed did I come to understand those words. It became crystal clear to me that my body was still functioning, and I was still alive—even though my creatinine level was sixteen, an unheard-of number for a creatinine level—because God is the core of my existence! He is the core of all our existence. He is our heartbeat, our breath, and any other major organ function. They function because of him. They function because of his grace and mercy. We live and we function because of *him*!

God's grace is his love in action! He continues to show us grace daily by providing us with the continuous breath of life. God's mercy is his unmerited favor. Its favor granted to us undeservingly. The unconditional love that God has for us causes him to extend his grace and his mercy to us. We have the obligation to extend these very same favors to others. When opportunities present themselves, and they often do, we should spring into action, demonstrating grace. When individuals need forgiving, have hurt you in some way, or have violated your trust, you are expected to extend mercy, for it was and is being extended to you daily, moment by moment.

I now know and understand that God extended and continues to extend his grace and mercy toward me because he has a work for me to finish. I believe that work includes sharing words of inspiration and encouragement. That work includes inspiring and building up others. That work includes demonstrating acts of love and kindness, regardless of who the person is and regardless of whether they are deserving of it or not. For I am not deserving of such unconditional love, bountiful grace, and unending mercies; however, these things have and continue to be extended toward me.

When faced with challenging situations in life, if it is related to your health or other matters, pause and pray. Ask the Lord, "What is my purpose? Have I fulfilled it?" If the answer to the latter is no, thank God for continued grace and mercy, which, if related to health, transforms into divine healing.

## Grace and Mercy Memento

Grace and mercy cannot be earned; however, demonstrating
and extending grace and mercy can be learned.

## Reflection Moment

Take a moment, sit quietly and still, listen to the voice of the Lord, and take note of what he is speaking to you right now regarding his grace and mercy. Reflect on past moments, how you responded, and what you can do differently going forward.

### Reflection Starters

Do I consistently forgive? Do I demonstrate God's unmerited favor?

Do I remind myself that I have been forgiven?

_____

_____

_____

_____

_____

_____

_____

_____

_____

## Scripture Moment

"For the LORD God is our sun and our shield. He gives us grace and glory. The LORD will withhold no good thing from those who do what is right." (Psalm 84:11)

"The LORD replied, 'I will make all my goodness pass before you, and I will call out my name, Yahweh, before you. For I will show mercy to anyone I choose, and I will show compassion to anyone I choose.'" (Exodus 33:19)

# MOMENT OF NEGATIVITY

Have you ever found yourself surrounded by negativity? Do you ever leave a conversation feeling deflated and drained? Do you ever feel bitter and angry, and after spending some time with a certain person or certain group of people, you leave with less energy than you started and full of negative thoughts?

We have all had these unfortunate experiences. Some of us live in the NE. What's the NE? The NE is negative energy, designed to block our blessings.

Do you ever find yourself looking forward to something, and you share that with a person who lives in the NE and suddenly, you are no longer expecting your blessing. Suddenly you are complaining about everything and everybody. Suddenly you find that you have elevated your natural circumstance to the point where your situation looks bigger than the God we serve!

Beware of the NE and the people who live for it. I have found that if you want to know how your future is going to look, take a long, hard look at the present company that you are keeping. Pay attention to the words and actions that individuals use. Pay attention to how people who live in the NE respond or react when you share good news, when you need to vent, when you are seeking encouragement, when you share how you are feeling, and so on. People who live in the NE have lived in it so long that they don't even recognize it, as it has become so natural for them. If you are not keenly aware, prayed up, and full of God's word, you too, my friend, will fall into the NE way of living.

What's the risk of living in the NE? What's at stake? Glad you asked. Your entire livelihood and way of living is at stake—not to mention the livelihood of those who are closest to you, those you admire, those who look up to you, and those who seek you out for advice, counsel and encouragement. Our influence simply influences. That's why it is critical that we are mindful of the words we use when we speak, for words carry energy. It is important for us to be mindful of how we react and respond to people and situations. Our energy matters, and the energy of those we spend a great deal of time around also matters. Want to change what's happening in your life? Change the people you are around, and change the words that you are speaking.

I challenge you to transition to the PE—positive energy—way of living, and I guarantee you that you will not regret it. I view most situations through a positive lens, as this helps me to get through whatever trial I am faced with. I believe life is about perspective, and that perspective is a choice. We choose how to view things, and we choose what type of energy we engage in and emit.

If you have been living in the NE, it's not too late to transition to the PE! From this very moment, watch over the words that you speak. Speak out into the universe what you desire to see come to pass. Challenge those around you who live in the NE to embrace the PE by modeling the behavior and challenging their NE by countering their words, thoughts, and perspectives with PE. Try it. It works.

## Negativity Memento

Alter your perspective to the positive and watch how differently you will see the things in the world. Life has a more pleasant scenery through the eyes of positivity.

# Reflection Moment

Take a moment, sit quietly and still, listen to the voice of the Lord, and take note of what he is speaking to you right now regarding negativity. Reflect on past moments, how you responded, and what you can do differently going forward.

## *Reflection Starters*

Do I engage in and enjoy negative talk? Do I counter negative talk with positive perspectives?

Does my circle of family and friends represent positive or negative energy?

_____

_____

_____

_____

_____

_____

_____

_____

_____

_____

## Scripture Moment

"The tongue can bring death or life; those who love to talk will reap the consequences." (Proverbs 18:21)

"And now, dear brothers and sisters, one final thing. Fix your thoughts on what is true, and honorable, and right, and pure, and lovely, and admirable. Think about things that are excellent and worthy of praise." (Philippians 4:8)

# MOMENT OF FRIENDSHIP

What is a friend? A friend is someone who loves you unconditionally, no questions asked. He or she is keenly aware of all your ways, the positives and the negatives. We are not taught how to be friends or how to conduct ourselves in a friendship. There are people in our lives who we naturally and spiritually connect with. We become friends, and our friendship evolves and blossoms over time.

A friend will be there when no one else is available. He or she will make sacrifices that no one else is willing to or even cares to make. We don't know why we became friends and often don't recall how;

we just are. We have connected on levels that we have not been able to with others. I believe this is by design. It is not meant for us to enter friendships with everyone. A true friendship is reserved for and designed for select individuals. I have heard people say, "Some people come into your life for a reason, a season, or a lifetime." A true friendship will last for a lifetime. Despite any time, lapse of talking, or seeing one another, despite any distance, friends will always be connected and are always there for one another. They are able to pick up where they last left off.

God made all living beings to be social creatures. We require love and companionship from others. Friends are there for the reasons, the seasons, and for the lifetime to provide that social connection that we all crave. These lifetimers may enter your life early or even later, but you will know them upon their arrival. They might come disguised as a mother, father, sister, brother, husband, wife, child, coworker, or someone you met while standing in line at the grocery store. However, one thing will stand out about a friend, and that is the unconditional, unselfish love and concern they show you even when you don't deserve it.

Have you ever experienced a true friendship? I am willing to bet you have. I am fortunate to have experienced this gift from a multitude of individuals: from a mother, from a sister, from people I have met in the workplace, and from my dear husband, James. I am so fortunate to have met my lifetime partner of over twenty years of marriage at a very young age. It was through our union that I gained my first reason to want to continue to live. James and I met during a very tumultuous time of my life. It was a time when I was feeling unworthy of living. I felt unloved and unwanted. I was mentally unhealthy, to put it bluntly. However, James loved me right through it all. He is a man of few words, but I recall twice in our marriage when he has spoken some profound words, which gave me hope. These words touched me in a way that I had never been touched before. I recall in 2008 being ill and near death, and he looked me in my eyes and said, "I want my wife back." I know that these words went from his mouth directly through my heart and into God's ears because God certainly honored his desire by bringing me back from death's door and raising me up to continue to our lifelong friendship.

It was through our union that I learned about another friendship, another friend, named Jesus. It was through our union that I came to learn that there was a perfect plan of not only salvation for me after this life, but that there was a plan for me right here on earth: a plan to prosper and to be of good health!

While our marriage seemed unconventional, I am confident that it was divinely orchestrated by God. My reason for sharing this moment of friendship is this: We sometimes miss our friendship moments. We sometimes miss our blessings and, thereby, our deliverance—not because they are unattainable, but because we are sometimes too restrictive in our thinking. We are apprehensive to show vulnerability and to be fully transparent. We have a vision or image in our minds regarding how our blessings should look, not realizing that our friend may show up as a male barely out of his teens, who has no money, no means of support, no relationship experience, no vision, nothing. This friend has nothing to offer but love. I am so happy that I was found in a vulnerable state. I am so happy that God loved me so much that he intervened by sending me my James, my husband. And over the years, he continued to intervene by sending me other friends and giving me other friendships to carry me through until the end of my journey. These special friends know me. They accept my shortcomings. They overemphasize my strengths. They support me through all my struggles. I am grateful for these friendships.

Ask yourself these questions and reflect: Who are my friends? What friendships am I nourishing? Have I turned away a special, life-altering blessing by being unwilling to make a new friend or to build a new friendship? Am I being the best friend that I can be to someone?

My prayer is that you have embraced friendship moments and that you will continue to do so, for they provide the opportunity to give the good parts of yourself to someone who is looking to be made whole through a friend.

## A Poem Pause

"Friendships Are"

Friendships are meant to stand the test of time. They are solid relationships comprised of trust, companionship, laughter, tears, and are forever being refined. They are not meant to be perfect, without ups and downs, but are available and present when there is no one else around.

Friendships should be treasured, relished, and nourished, for they are few, far, and in between, some insincere, not meant to flourish. Friendships are designed for life situations that sometimes throw us, but we can count on that friendship if it is genuine and robust. So, take the time to invest in a friend, so that when your life or their life comes to an end, you both know, without a shadow of a doubt, that you were indeed true friends.

## **Friendship Memento**

Friendships are special connections intended for special
people who have been divinely introduced.

## Reflection Moment

Take a moment, sit quietly and still, listen to the voice of the Lord, and take note of what he is speaking to you right now regarding friendships. Reflect on past moments, how you responded, and what you can do differently going forward.

### *Reflection Starters*

Have I been a true friend to someone?

Am I open to making new friends?

_____

_____

_____

_____

_____

_____

_____

_____

_____

_____

## Scripture Moment

"The seeds of good deeds become a tree of life; a wise person wins friends." (Proverbs 11:30)

"Here's the lesson: Use your worldly resources to benefit others and make friends. Then, when your earthly possessions are gone, they will welcome you to an eternal home." (Luke 16:9)

# A Concluding Moment

I hope you have found this inspirational journal to be inspiring. The moments shared in this writing are the most prominent moments that came to mind. They seem to be the most universal that we all share and have experienced at some point in our lives.

This book was designed to be used often, to review repeatedly and as often as needed. It is intended to stir up the stirrer in you. It is intended to highlight and remind you that you are more than a conqueror! It is intended to remind you of the original plan and promises that God left on record for us and how we can apply those promises to our everyday moments. It is intended to provide a simplistic, down-to-earth, everyday kind of practical, living examples to help you to connect to and hold fast to the Word of God.

I hope that the insertions of my personal stories helped to bring the intentions of the messages home. If nothing else, it demonstrates that we are all the same. We all experience the same thoughts, emotions, and moments. The unique and distinguishing difference is how we choose to respond.

If you have a moment and you would like me to expand upon something that was not addressed in this book, reach out to me and let me know. I will pause, pray, and wait for the whisper of the Lord and document the words of inspiration that he gives. And I will share those moments in the next series of *Moments*.

Thank you for taking a moment to be inspired.

# Rhoda's Mementos

*These sayings, also found at the end of each Moment reflection reading, are enduring words spoken directly from God's mouth to my ears. I affectionately refer to them as Rhoda's Mementos and have provided them here for ease in reference. You are encouraged to reflect upon, delight in, and use these words for ongoing encouragement and inspiration for yourself and others.*

**Moment of Hope:** Hope is not helpless. It is full of optimistic strength, making the unbelievable achievable.

**Moment of Fear:** Fear is unbelief in disguise.

**Moment of Truth:** If you are not doing anything in the Lord, not doing anything to further the truth, not doing anything to help and to develop people and their faith, then you are not doing anything at all.

**Moment of Despair:** Despair is a natural emotion. To embrace it, to foster it, and to accept it is unnatural and leads to even greater despair.

**Moment of Joy:** True joy may seem unobtainable to some; to those who believe this, it is.

**Moment of Strength:** Strength and faith are companions for endurance.

**Moment of Love:** The substitute for love is nonexistent, and unconditional love loves despite the return on investment.

**Moment of Rejection:** The act of rejection is seeded and rooted with a cunning and evil plot; however, the act of rejecting rejection has the power to deplete, destroy, and supersede its ultimate plan.

**Moment of Happiness:** Happiness and peace are connected, and their bonds are unbreakable. You can't have one without the other.

**Moment of Frustration:** Frustration is a matter of reaction in the heat of a moment. Trust and faith in God are matters that deliver in every moment and every time.

**Moment of Victory:** Victory is only attained and sustained through the power of God.

**Moment of Confidence:** A confident man is a man of faith. An arrogant man is a man of unbelief.

**Moment of Inspiration:** Go inspire, for an uninspired person is consumed and destroyed by despair.

**Moment of Grief and Sorrow:** Grief and sorrow are cousins, holding hands, but joy and peace are present and available to help you to withstand. Choose your companions.

**Moment of Encouragement:** Encouraging others is the secret to encouraging one's own self.

**Moment of Grace and Mercy:** Grace and mercy cannot be earned. However, demonstrating and extending grace and mercy can be learned.

**Moment of Negativity:** Alter your perspective to the positive and watch how differently you will see the things in the world. Life has a much more pleasant scenery through the eyes of positivity.

**Moment of Friendship:** Friendships are special connections intended for special people who have been divinely introduced.

# Your Afterthoughts

Use this section to note any additional thoughts and words inspired by God from reading this devotional. What will you do differently or more of going forward?

_____

_____

_____

_____

_____

_____

_____

_____

_____

_____

_____

_____

_____

_____

_____

_____

_____

_____

_____

## Author Biography

Rhoda Banks is a born-again believer who grew up in a low-income housing project in the inner city of St. Louis, Missouri. She is the oldest of four siblings, raised by a single mother. Rhoda worked her way through school, earning a Bachelor of Arts in Business Administration, a Master's in Human Resource Training and Development, and a Master's in Healthcare Administration. She makes her living as an executive in human resources and serves as a part-time adjunct professor. Rhoda is passionate about others, has a genuine love and concern for people in general, and gives back through volunteerism and individual mentoring and coaching, positively impacting the lives of many, one by one. Rhoda is known as a "glass half full" type of person, known for mottos such as "all things are temporary," and, "to every problem, there is a solution." Rhoda's can-do attitude and faith in God is both infectious and inspiring. Rhoda and her husband, James, have been married for more than two decades and are the parents of two sons. They make their home in Lake St. Louis, Missouri.